To Wish You Well in a Time of Healing

SUSAN SQUELLATI FLORENCE

Bristol Park Books

First Bristol Park Books edition published in 2017

Bristol Park Books
252 West 38th Street
New York, NY 10018

Bristol Park Books is a registered trademark
of Bristol Park Books, Inc.

Library of Congress Control Number:2017938927

ISBN:978-0-88486-659-6

E-Book ISBN:978-0-88486-660-2

Text and cover design by Keira McGuinness
Cover art copyright ©2017 Kristina Horina/Shutterstock

Printed in Malaysia

To:

_____

From:

_____

What matters

most in your

time of healing

is you.

The busy ways of life—

the endless lists of things to do,

the pressure and stress

of having to get it all done—

will stop.

It's a time to let go,

a time to rest, to take it easy,

a time to take it slow.

Healing can turn your life

upside-down.

Instead of helping others,

you are asked to "receive."

You will learn how important

and comforting it is to receive

kindnesses and love from friends,

family, and caregivers.

Their acts of caring—

the novel sent by a friend,

the savory soup a neighbor leaves by,

people calling to ask, "How are you?"

—will hearten you as you heal.

And yet, even as you feel this great gift

of connection with others. . .

you may sense how alone you are,

how fragile and mysterious is this place

you hold in the universe.

And you may wonder, "Why me?"

This time

of healing

is a journey.

You may travel to places

you never visited before

where you meet unspoken fears,

and climb mountains that rise up

inside yourself.

You may feel stranded in the unknowing,

like being lost in the wilderness

and not able to see

what lies ahead.

You may cry the deep sobs

of the earth and rage like rain

until the house around your heart

is cleansed.

Your feelings may change

like the shapes of white clouds

shifting in blue sky.

You may feel vulnerable, overwhelmed,

emotionally undone.

Yet new awarenesses

can come

in a time

of healing.

Even as you rely on and listen to others,

as they offer advice and suggestions,

you will begin to understand the messages

from your own body

and listen to what it says.

31

Your own body has a profound intuition

of what you need to heal.

In infinitesimal ways of being

you may feel changes unknown to others.

Your body will tell you how important

your energy is to healing,

when it is best to be alone,

when it is time to rest.

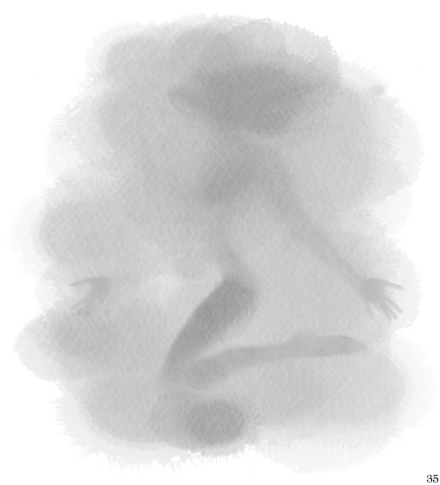

Your body may tell you that the best thing

you can do for yourself—

is nothing.

And in doing nothing you discover

that you are more than what you do.

Even when you are doing nothing—

you are you.

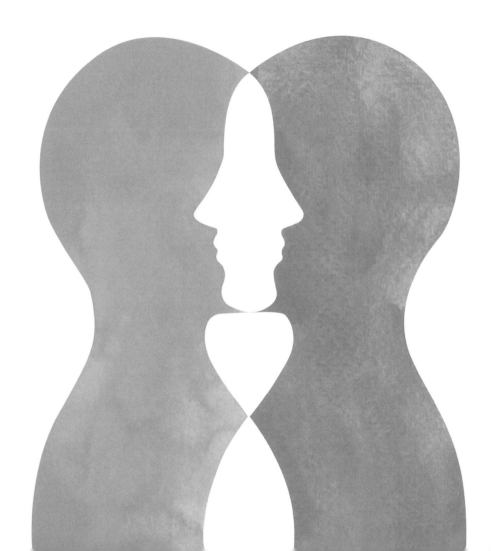

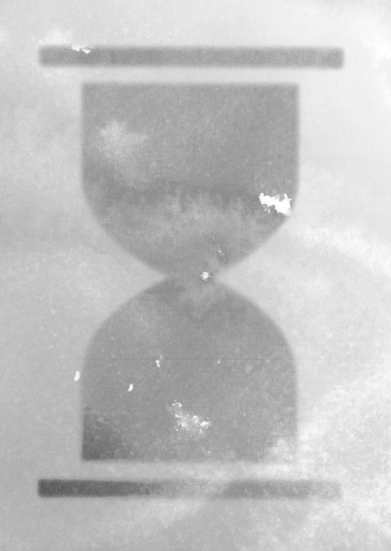

Everything,

especially healing,

has its own timing.

Your healing will take as long as it takes.

To compare your healing time with

another's is useless.

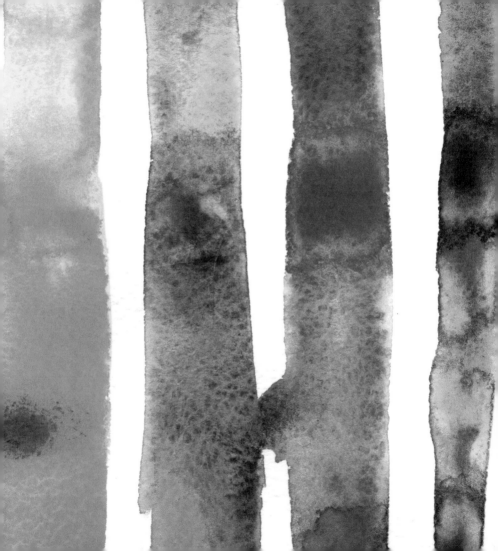

May contentment come to you

in this healing time.

May you realize it is not how much

you want from life

but how much you already have.

An absence of longing

and your surrender to the healing process

will lessen your worry

and aid in your healing.

May each day bring you

the wisdom that grows

as you develop a pathos for others,

knowing how much we all endure

on our different journeys—

knowing how much we matter

to each other.

We are all humbled and vulnerable

when we are in unknowing times.

We are fragile yet strong,

afraid yet brave,

unsure yet hopeful.

Your own positive thoughts

can help you when you can say,

"I am full of well being.

I am supported.

I am loved.

I grow stronger, day by day."

By choosing love and calm and joy

inside yourself

you can be at ease

as you are restored.

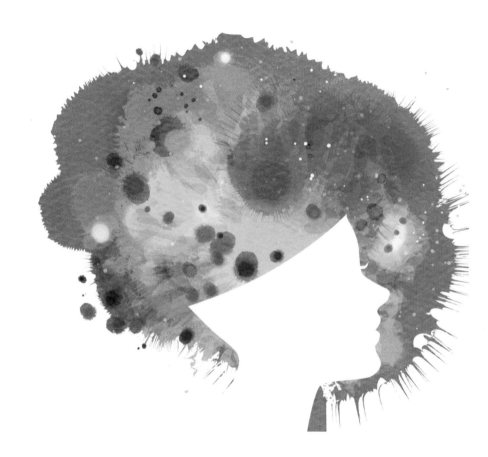

By choosing love and calm and joy

you are choosing the power

of good thoughts to help you heal.

May each dawn awaken in you

a new day of growing stronger.

May nature's beauty

and its changes

inspire you...

...to trust the oak tree that lives

in the acorn,

the butterfly that grows in the chrysalis,

the wisteria's fragrant flowers opening

from Spring's first pale buds.

May nature and its gifts help you to gain

an awareness of all things

that need time

to wait, to grow, to become.

May time itself

ripen into an abundant gift...

...time to stop and notice the sun's rays

that sparkle

through the windows of your life,

time to really listen to another,

time to move slowly through the day,

grateful for the gift

of a wildflower bouquet.

As you heal

life will pull you back

into its churning vortex of lists, and plans,

and things to do

today, tomorrow, next week, next month,

next year.

As you heal

life will call you back

to its cacophony of distractions

and noise.

But you can stop—

as others run around you—

and remember how it feels to be quiet,

how to be still.

How it feels to watch the sunlight turn

an afternoon amber spreading gold

through the branches of bamboo.

You can stop and remember

the gifts of care and kindness

from people who believe in you,

from those who are ever-there for you,

whose flow of love helps you heal.

May the support, caring thoughts and love

you receive remain with you

and enrich your days

long after your healing time.

Illustration Credits